Haiku?
No— MyKu!

A Poetry Collection

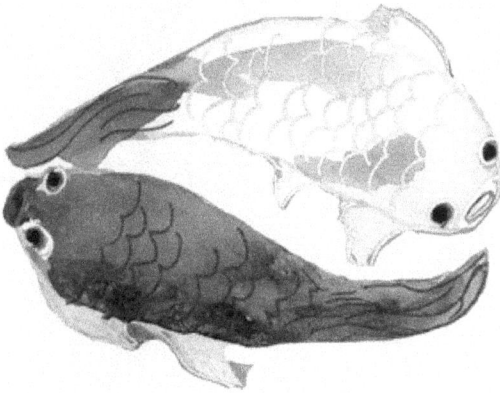

BY

TANYA RICHEY

DEDICATION

Without family, friends, neighbors and
strangers a person is nothing.
Without patrons, experiences, and risks
an artist starves.

Here's to the ebb and the flow
and the hungry spirits we come to know.

Doing what I do
Painting down my naked roots
Dabbling round the earth

CONTENTS

タツヤ

エイプリル

冬

WINTER

Snowy soft mountains

Below a mellow sunset

Contemplate, create

MYKU 1

Christmas is over
Sunset on the Kanto Plain
The sky is open

MYKU 2

Sagami River
It flows but does not return
As it was before

MYKU 2

Winter, cold wind bites
Rosy blossoms confusing
Sazaka watching

MYKU 4

I art by daylight
Ponder Japan awkwardly
Into night softly

MYKU 5

In search of order
Misty coldness out my window
The new year coming

MYKU 6

I look at the moon
The moon hangs in the new year
We look at the new moon

MYKU 7

Take life as it comes
The new year moon looks at us
Up the tree bugs crawl

MYKU 8

Round white moon
Rain and mist over the fence
The dog stares ahead

MYKU 9

Cold gloomy morning
Cooking chard, red veins dazzle
Winter withering

MYKU 10

Where go the dark birds
In windy silence they fly
I sit alone

MYKU 11

The warm orange sun
Over the leftover snow
Where does your heart lie

MYKU 12

Walk to the temple
Burn new year's rope and pine, *hai*
Let go of last year

MYKU 13

Like an animal
Drawn to that one patch of sun
Still, happiness comes

MYKU 14

FU YU GO MO RI
Shuttering in, bundling-
up, keeping warm, soup

MYKU 15

Still winter light
Thinking the questions out loud
My bare toes are cold

MYKU 16

Rosy dawn appeared
Quick to eat the evening star
Obligatory

MYKU 17

Yamabushi sun
Painting, an act of worship
Pass through and enter

MYKU 18

Grilling fish riverside
Appreciating fresh air
Warmth, pleasure invade

MYKU 19

Morning dog walking
White sky, drizzle, pale, shadows
Cut through delusion

MYKU 20

Gray out my window
Can this be "the middle way"
Thoughts come and thoughts go

MYKU 21

Winter green, inside
Intrusive ambivalence
Leaf, water, light, life

MYKU 22

Think about what's gone
Or think about what's here
The pale sun breaks through

MUKU 23

All things can be yours
If you keep them in your mind
White clouds, blue skies, us

MYKU 24

For the time being
Waiting for winter to pass
A light on the bowl

MYKU 25

Red petals poke out
White clumps of snow holding on
Diligent time passes

MYKU 26

Drip, drip, drip, splash, splat
Sit and wait or meditate
The snow is melting

MYKU 27

Daruma help me.
Fall down seven times, get up eight
Full moon, yearning hand

MYKU 28

Completely blue sky
Walk to the old temple
A bench in the sun

MYKU 29

When old age comes
Every day is a journey
Cold wind at your back

MYKU 30

Smoke drifts over me
Pray for a seat on the train
Bare trees winter streets

MYKU 31

Mt Fuji-san view
Tokyo, a morning moon
Setsubun over

MYKU 32

Winter nothingness
My head is filled with thoughts
Sardines swimming by

MYKU 33

A winter day
The black shawl hangs on the chair
Possibilities

MYKU 34

Gray rain transcending
Best way to honor the dead
Cherish the living

MYKU 35

Shadow of Fuji
Spring strolling amid the crowds
East, West, Shop, shop, shops

MYKU 36

Through clouds salient
February mountain snow
Soon blossoms to come

MYKU 37

Boats bob in sunset
Water cleanses the spirit
First view of Fuji

MYKU 38

Like the first blossom
Bursting forth from the bare tree
Good friends warm my heart

MYKU 39

To write vernally
Hiragana, line, curve, dot
Katakana, frog

MYKU 40

Thinking and acting
Again trying to balance
Painting through the clouds

15

MYKU 41

Longing Connection
Early spring pussy willows
Life smolders within

MYKU 42

Morning after snow
Resolutions on my mind
Tea water is hot

MYKU 43

Old dreams of the past
The insistent cold spring rain
Youth dream the future

MYKU 44

It is in our minds
So that is where we must search
Spring rain dulls the light

MYKU 45

In urban confines
A need to transport oneself
To a still calm place

MYKU 46

Light makes the snow pink
He who knows nothing is wise
Great capacity

MYKU 47

An almost warm month
Remember all the presidents
Prime ministers too

MYKU 48

It's not where you are
But what you do while you're there
Sunny day dry out

MYKU 49

Clean, draw, paint, love, smile
White clouds in listening skies
It is what it is

MYKU 50

Drizzle gray feet rain
Know nothing of immortal
Make this life worth while

MYKU 51

Fog, sun, quake, rain, night
First make plan then take action
Re-evaluate

MYKU 52

No hot cold simple
Sunlight shafts revealing dust
Hanging in the air

MYKU 53

Spring cleaning observed
Preparation, gathering
Select, purify

MYKU 54

Bright cloudy aura
Refresh the spirit each day
Thoughts of spring blossoms

MYKU 55

Rain, Light, Rain, Rain, Showers
Old attachment flow behind
Away dust and grime

MYKU 56

February wanes
Racing raindrops follow chase
Trees swollen with buds

MYKU 57

Still cold buy incense
Fan smoke toward stiff body
Rough start to New Year

MYKU 61

The last winter moon
Pink clouds, flexibility
One wave in great ocean

MYKU 63

Each day good of bad
A decision you can make
Let the sun inside

MYKU 64

Clouds crawl over Truth
I art therefore I am
Sitting in the sunshine

MYKU 65

Rise full moon–Crow Moon
Insistent caws heralding
The end of winter

MYKU 66

In the distant haze
Fundamental nothingness
This thought penetrates

MYKU 67

Spring pushes through time
Releasing new energy
Invigorated

MYKU 68

As it is it is
Passionate concentration
Blue water old hills

MYKU 69

In the vast blue sky
Your Universe is waiting
Sit alone and seek

MYKU 70

I am an artist
Flowing constantly searching
Master of nothing

MYKU 71

On the verge of rain
I can see no gate ahead
The patch is slippery

MYKU 72

Bask in warm spring sun
Come summer we will seek shade
Sit awhile have tea

MYKU 73

Without agenda
Luminous cloudy cold day
A noble person

MYKU 74

Parsley rosemary
Smiling Buddha among rocks
Lucky in the sun

MYKU 75

The bright sun is loud
The temple bell is silent
Nearly squawking birds

MYKU 76

Backyard in Japan
Blue Flowers, grass and clover
Somethings are the same

MYKU 77

Don't know where I am
Spring when the sun pushes through
So I am not lost

MYKU 78

Winter losing ground
Gray mountain coming forward
Sit and wait calmly

MYKU 79

Purple cloud passes
The March wind gathers no moss
Blue mountain appears

Even monkeys fall from the trees

春

SPRING

Wispy willow tree

The calligraphy of spring

Writing down the limbs

MyKu 80

Ever-changing clouds
March ends Cherry blossoms start
Months come and months go

MyKu 81

Create quality
Whatever means are at hand
Do come and sit first

MYKU 82

Perplexing gray sky
Thinking is overrated
Softly soaking rain

MYKU 83

Blossoms in the air
Bare to bud and back again
Notice in between

MYKU 84

Cold winter drizzle
March brings April rain showers
April rain, storms brew

MYKU 85

Snow among the rain
Difficult to reconcile
Get the coat back out

MYKU 86

Rain, wind, clouds, crowds, cold
Cherry Blossom Festival
Realm of sights, sounds, smells

MYKU 87

Light rain brings rebirth
Blossoms giving way to leaves
Vital procession

MYKU 88

Enveloped in mist
Cyclic intentions fulfilled
Faded blossoms drop

MYKU 89

Sun searching through fog
Find your own way to center
Original source

MYKU 90

Affords tedium
Indoors in sunshine waste day
Walk outside the gate

MYKU 91

Emerged to meet needs
Stratus of low-lying clouds
Lose vitality

MYKU 92

To paint one painting
Direct perception of view
Lifetime of seeing

MYKU 93

From clouds darts the sun
The energy circulates
Pacifies the mind.

MYKU 94

Practical drawing
Logical coherent form
Magical results

MYKU 95

Initiated
Spring slipping in between clouds
Rain latent within

MYKU 96

Small green dogwood buds
Gently emerge along limbs
Clouds fold into air

MYKU 97

Paper white dogwoods
Intrinsic part of the heart
Sagacious April

MYKU 98

April rain again
Dandelions everywhere
Weeds cut through the ground.

MYKU 99

Sake and sushi
Inscrutable is Japan
martini and fish

MYKU 100

A clear April day
Accept and change
move and learn
Engage and create

MYKU 101

A clear day, clear mind,
Face in, Face out, remove all
Prepare for fresh start

MYKU 102

April continues
Raining all the dull day long
Treasure sword in hand

MYKU 103

Use the sacred sword
within us eliminate
April's spent blossoms

MYKU 104

If you want to learn
Truly let go, know nothing
Can the sky be blue

29

MYKU 105

May came in warmly
I know what I said
But not what you heard

MYKU 106

Emphasize progress
Remember preservation
Show development

MYKU 107

Learn the rules then wait
Exceptions soon to follow
Sun today then rain

MYKU 108

Same bush one red bloom
Among all the white blossoms
Japanese studies

MYKU 109

Let us drink and laugh
Across the oceans times fly
New memories lie

MYKU 110

Watch for side currents
An unmoored boat drifts away
Beware hot loose talk

MYKU 111

Dust from the shadows
Fresh breeze moves serene bamboo
Faded vermilion

MYKU 112

Fish market shopping
Big mackerel heads, flattened squid
Dead fish, live people

MYKU 113

Look forward walk back
Ancient gingko tree is green
Look backward walk front

MYKU 114

Ageless noble pine
Stand and enjoy the raindrops
Brother of my heart

MYKU 115

Heaven has no gate
Remember earth has no door
Not your tree in rain

MYKU 116

May's golden bamboo
Nor bowing respectfully
Time to harvest tea

MYKU 117

Eighty-eight nights pass
Pokka-dotted tea pickers
Roam in neat green rows

MYKU 118

Task well done, good day
Straw hats, happy tea jackets
Almost summer time

MYKU 119

Tea grown in shadows
Brings light into a dark room
Transcending venture

MYKU 120

Green tea basket full
Savor the life in your cup
Prevent intrusion

MYKU 121

Sunshine sprinkled on
Freshly picked green tea leaves
Breathe deep easily

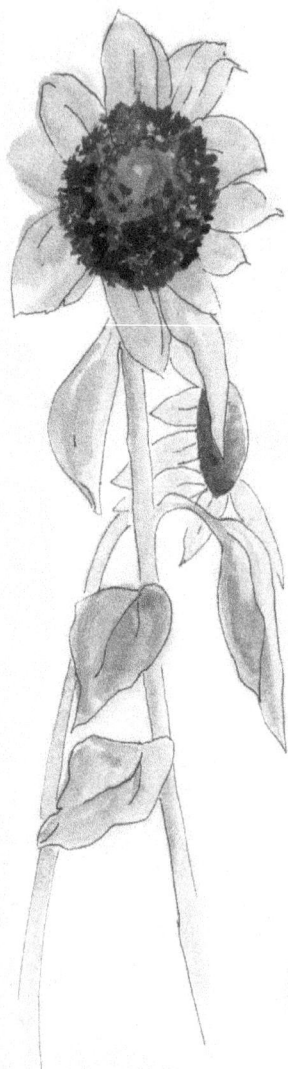

夏

SUMMER

Indecisiveness

Soon the clouds will drift away

Right before your eyes

MYKU 352

Kabuki with Friends
Drums beat song sing, costumes move
Tokyo in June

MYKU 122

Once a fat plum tree
Now nearly, poor, old and fat.
A happy Buddha.

MYKU 123

Ueno Park man
Standing motionless– pensive
Flitting sparrows perch

MYKU 124

Traveling poet
May day talk in city square
"I hate these people"

MYKU 125

Close air, tempers rise
All fall short of the glory
of the card, write on.

MYKU 126

Lady bird dancer
Latin rhythms in the air
White crane in lily pads

MYKU 127

Shrine fox, fierce eyes
White papers hang earnest prayers
The summer ebbs in

MYKU 128

Standing on the train
A sea of humanity
Ocean of buildings

MYKU 129

Murky creatures rise
Fighting dismal gray clouds
Wave reflections bounce

MYKU 130

Hovering low tide
Mt. Fuji is the weather
It is always there

MYKU 131

Words fall from the sky
Azure promises good ideas
Tumbling from my head

MYKU 132

Where does the road go
The path reaches every port
Short cuts, only one

MYKU 133

Life can be revealed
Sitting by the sea with poll
But never explained

MYKU 134

Do not complicate
The sea is so vast and wide
Why ask why exist

MYKU 135

Boats probe the water
Harbor houses keep vigil
Gulls break the silence

MYKU 135b

Fall down hand meets ground
Fire sunsets, black mountains
Pop back up

MYKU 136

The sun comes out loud
To get something today
You must do something
good now

MYKU 137

Clouds drag by slowly
So I thought life was to be
Vanity of earth by things

MYKU 138

Squandering raindrops
Ten pensive days of long rain
earth is wet enough

MYKU 139

Down to Togo cove
Making the journey of life
Just enough baggage

MYKU 140

Perched with daylilies
Looking into green water
Small octopi swim

MYKU 141

View nature alone
Look at paintings in the dark
Clouded over June

MYKU 142

Count moments not days
And you will have time enough
Wax impartially

MYKU 143

Vines, miles behind
Filtered by motion
Glad true in full greens

MYKU 144

Clouds swallow mountains
Villages become cities
Tangles eat fences

MYKU 145

Your intuition should
Be tempered with knowledge
Hot summer solstice

MYKU 146

Altair herds cattle
Way across the Milky Way
Vega weaves fine cloth

MYKU 147

Hot July morning
Gathering dew to make ink
Don't let the cows out

MYKU 148

Hanging Bamboo
Wishes on colored paper
Neglecting weaving

MYKU 149

On one clear warm night
Capriciousness awaits us
Meeting once again

MYKU 150

Fellow travelers
Sleeping, making plans, talking
Stars across the sky

MYKU 151

Rainy season ends
Surviving hot period
Summer sweltering

MYKU 152

Mid-summer *shochu*
Greetings in lingering heat
Take a little pause

MYKU 153

Enjoy the summer
Unrelieved sobriety
Is itself excess

MYKU 154

There is worth within
The humblest of hedges
The fox is hunting

MYKU 155

Lacquer dries slowly
In humid, sticky, hot air
Tedious and dull.

MYKU 156

We can only hope
to have things our way awhile
Future made from past

MYKU 157

Attachment to things
An old gate still holds me back
Dark with ancient trees

MYKU 158

All the little fishes
In the summer sea, swim round
and round hopefully

MYKU 159

Healthy rabbit food
Oh, that I could embrace it
In the August heat

MYKU 160

Relentless white sun
Hot and damp no stirring air
Cool rain is welcome

MYKU 161

Dancing in the night
Colors pulsing everywhere
August festival

MYKU 162

Will the heat subside
The current of the years runs
In one direction.

MYKU 163

Moonless joyful night
of dark gentle sultry charm
Lighted sky above

MYKU 164

Buggy muggy night
Don't let the world steal your joy
Not friends, kin or foe

MYKU 165

Dark trees dark mountains
People shinning voices loud
Leading families home.

MYKU 166

Path for starving ghosts
A great moon beyond the gate
Night of illusion

MYKU 167

Human song and dance
Drowns out the crickets' concert
Though they both go on

MYKU 168

Summer and brass bands
That call such sweet music forth
Linger in the mind

MYKU 169

Laughter and voices
Heat abating wafting breeze
Vying memories

45

MYKU 170

Moon lets in spirits
Finish your own melody
Encroaching shadows

MYKU 171

Are the old tunes good
Are they deep, profound, honest
Or just familiar

MYKU 172

Does our ear reject
Stirring sound we don't know
Middle August rain

MYKU 350

Augmenting the night
The band's passionate ardor
Evanescent sound

MYKU 173

A few yellow leaves
Gray clabbered sky fleeting on
Hints of what's to come

MYKU 174

Evanescent years
Losing meaning as they go
Mask reveals torments

MYKU 175

Is life black or gray
Brush and the sword are the same
White sky in morning

MYKU 176

Sooner or later
Through wind or rainy seasons
We are all alone

MYKU 176b

Troubles of the day
May dissolve in the blithe of night
Lovely crescendo

MYKU 177

Shades of happiness
Sunsets bold and beautiful
The night encroaches

MYKU 178

Final phase, decline
Sun's daily disappearance
Rapturously we rest

MYKU 179

Many interpretations
Philosophy comes easy
Just begin again

MYKU 180

Rain makes sunflowers
Vegetables and sake
Disaffected thoughts

MYKU 181

People will take naps
When one has thoughts on their mind
Some emotions fade

MYKU 182

Hot days, hotter nights
This world produces trifles
August is their month

MYKU 183

Happy position
Not too burdened with glory
Obsequious speech

MYKU 184

Elegance and grace
Can push admiration to
the point of envy

MYKU 185

Away from the world
You may run impulsively
Ominous rumblings

MYKU 186

Violent rain squall
The mood as black as the sky
Mutability

MYKU 187

Straight forward sunflower
Hot breeze among the grasses
Go unencumbered

MYKU 188

Tanuki pops up
Looking for his sake jug
Zama sunflowers

MYKU 189

My momma told me
Do not fatten frogs for snakes
Summer rolls along

MYKU 190

Thick heat in air
The ending of summer is near
Regard with resolve

MYKU 191

Hard sound of raindrops
Freedom from binding regrets
Morning now evening

MYKU 192

Pouring rain comes down
Of originality
Are the words so thick

MYKU 193

Brass bells, books and beads
Praying, studying, sitting
Consequently

MYKU 194

Sticks in heavy hair
The things we do for fashion
September Rain Song

MYKU 195

September came in
on a dark cloud of despair
Shifting attention

MYKU 196

Taste without chewing
Make up your mind call it fate
Return to artwork

MYKU 197

Go cross the river
Through long tunnel meet mountains
New season begins

MYKU 198

Rain-laden anger
The typhoon number eighteen
Thunderbolt

MYKU 199

Then a storm came down
On top of the stone foxes
Spotted all over

MYKU 200

Exuberant rain
Reflect on what time has done
Raindrop by raindrop

MYKU 201

I am not learning
Much of anything by talking
Close door on summer

MYKU 202

Sitting and walking
New season, a new reason
And the game plays on

MYKU 203

Leaves twist in the wind
Money and time same effort
Result inherent

MYKU 204

Investment in time
Wet blotches on the pathway
Heading to the train

MYKU 205

Damp cedar forest
To see the world vividly
Allow mystery

MYKU 206

Clouds melt into trees
To over-value reason
Shrinks the greenest moss

MYKU 207

Stumble hesitate
Wet stones underneath my feet
Above leaves tremble

MYKU 208

A hint of coldness
Water splashes on my feet
The train home in near

MYKU 209

A garden pot sits
On the porch an empty chair
Gravel in my shoe

MYKU 210

Fire, fire, burn
Into the last light walking
Bells among voices

MYKU 211

Thoughts in my head fade
Fuji Fire Festival
Summer lost to time

MYKU 212

Fanciful group clothes
Students milling around grounds
Enjoying their youth

MYKU 213

While calmly kneeling
Whisk the tea at lightning speed
The room is silent

MYKU 214

Ink splashes forward
The body retreats backward
Words hit the paper

MYKU 215

Silent corridor
Large empty room town outside
Brushes in window

MYKU 216

Interior view
A sunset begins morning
Walk outwardly on

MYKU 217

Various colors
Grasses and berries abound
Early fall viewing

MYKU 218

Enclosed from town
By stately looming old trees
The shrine entices

MYKU 219

The incense burning
Quiet light on the statue
I pick up a stone

MYKU 220

Red dogwood berries
The beginning of autumn
The days are shorter

MYKU 221

Obscure gray buildings
Tiled roofs hanging heavily
Faces look at me

MYKU 222

An uncertain sky
There will be no moon viewing
But much good sleeping

秋

AUTUMN

Autumn falls on us

The ground is now colorful

Leaves scatter our thoughts

MYKU 175b

Fall sun, hats needed
Squat and bend tending flowers
I have had gardens

MYKU 223

Sitting eating lunch
Gazing out the large window
A few red leaves call

MYKU 224

The first cautious step
Out the door into autumn
With everyone else

MYKU 225

Along the walkway
The flattened wet yellow leaves
I see the big frog

MYKU 226

Do not let me die
Unenlightened and yearning
In a foreign land

MYKU 227

Appetite unchecked
Prisoner of my own making
Standing in puddles

MYKU 228

Colors of Genji
His nocturnal wandering
A book of Japan

MYKU 229

Wakas much weeping
Death, gods invoked continue
Life's experience

MuKu 230

Through fans and curtains
One of many flowers strewn
In the royal court

MYKU 231

The Heian Court lives,
Once more in dolls girls play with.
Hinamatsuri

MYKU 232

Cold wind at-his-back
An Emperor faces south
To survey his realm

MYKU 233

Glorious fabrics
Her majesty the Empress
She needs a stiff neck

MYKU 234

Watching the sky
Not a turtle nor a crane
I'll live till I die

MYKU 235

Characters make words
City is many buildings
Many people too

MYKU 236

Out of my window
I saw a bright supermoon
Emerge from the clouds

61

MYKU 237

The man in the moon
A rabbit pounding *mochi*
All is perspective.

MYKU 238

Black nebulous clouds
Scattered and eclipsed the moon
I doze off to dream

MYKU 239

I hear word of it
The first snow in the mountains
But the sun shines here

MYKU 240

Happenings in nights
Summon spirits cautiously
Stir up lesser gods

MYKU 241

Lightning through the night
Rain hitting the window pain
The voice of thunder

MYKU 242

The morning after
The leaves hung on all night long
Stillness fills the air

MYKU 243

Leaves still on the trees
Thirtieth of September
Yellow mixed with green

MYKU 244

A warm zephyr sings
Giving fire rein to hopefulness
New inspiration

MYKU 245

Japanese garden
Perfection through artifice
Assimilation

MYKU 246

Goodbye September
Get out socks and turtle necks
Hello October

MYKU 247

October begins
Swirling black shadows
Moving filigree

MYKU 248

Rest is much sweeter
After some purposeful work
My hands are wrinkled

MYKU 249

Huddled in blankets
I know why it's called a cold
Because I'm freezing

MYKU 250

Now I am warm but
my nose is red and drippy
Moaning soothes the soul

MYKU 251

Leaves splotched with color
Spiderwebs of black branches
Transitory forms

MYKU 252

Now in a brown pile
I remember these spring leaves
To all autumn comes

MYKU 253

Freak of nature
Or an ordinary twig
Clings to life the same

MYKU 254

Reward is not here
What are we preparing for
Blue sky overhead

MYKU 255

Approaching fall skies
Speak to my wandering heart
Seek the middle way

MYKU 256

Earth, sky, much hard work
Live mindfully to receive
Food moderately

MYKU 257

On a calm gray day
A stream of consciousness flows
Everything the same

MYKU 258

The decline begins
Pay your toll and move forward
The gate opens wide

MYKU 353

The days grow shorter
Persimmons fall from the trees
Hearts begin to drift

MYKU 261

Autumn in Japan
Actually, life dries, spirit soars
Smell the persimmons

MYKU 262

Thick clouds had gathered
Hills disappeared into the gloom
The statues stand still

MYKU 263

Money in their hands
The rain obscured everything
Except the small coins

MYKU 264

Weeping bitter tears
My heart beats, my eyes see
My ears hear the rain

MYKU 265

A shaft of sunlight
Mounts the stone and creeps upward
Resting on bright leaves

MYKU 266

Sweet autumn fragrance
Benign assimilation
Dappling the shrine ground

MYKU 267

Down near the river
The heavier the rice stalk
The lower its head

MYKU 268

Harvest finale
Reaped rice leaning against poles
Drying in the sun

MYKU 269

Nuts drop from the trees
Soon the rice fields will be dry
Mark the occasion

MYKU 270

Opportunistic
Bevy of birds flock, frogs jump
Welcome windfall feast

MYKU 271

Red bats overhead
Blessings be vast as the sky
Feet shuffling leaves

MYKU 272

Five bats five blessings
Long life, wealth, health and virtue
Die natural death

MYKU 273

The days are still warm
Leaves rest on granite gravestones
Ancestors talking

MYKU 274

Strong, proud, who are they
The wind will take us away
Nights turning colder

MYKU 275

Pulled from the black dirt
Onions must grow everywhere
I like them in soup

MYKU 276

Autumn is soup time
Fresh bread, vegetables
Simmering slowly

MYKU 277

Angry foxes guard
Shinto shrines with twisted trees
mustard seed gardens

MYKU 278

Observing steward
Gray grainy stone animals
Alert ears hear all

MYKU 279

Rock hard sinews taunt
Faded red bibs around necks
Every minute strong

MYKU 280

Beyond this entrance
No evil intruders dwell
Continuous peace

MYKU 281

Presiding over
No senescence infinity
Autumn's pale sunlight

MYKU 282

Dictated by forms
Painting is nature recalled
In tranquility

MYKU 283

Brushed sinuous lines
Emotion revisited
The camellias bloom

MYKU 284

Lost in summers' dream
Drying, fading hydrangeas
Keep their plum blush

MYKU 285

Autumn colored fruit
Hanging heavy on the branch
Waiting to fall down

MYKU 286a

Soon to be eaten
Ripe persimmons huddle tight
Their leaves are spotted

MYKU 286b

Fall hangs in the air
Simple elegant gesture
My sweater is warm

MYKU 287a

Maple leaves turn red
In the rain last night some fell
Down I picked them up

MYKU 287b

Pressed against the asphalt
Flat with stems pointing upward
Easy to pick up

MYKU 288

My heart was happy
Enjoying nature is peace
When the mind lets go

MYKU 289

A day in the park
Families talking, bugs crawl
Blue sky and water

MYKU 290

Red leaves in autumn
Look there is the grass, mushrooms
Change makes us grow stronger

MYKU 291

Greens fading to thoughts
Idleness has purpose
A leaf in the wind

MYKU 292

Swift flowing water
Light stones along the river
White wings passing by

MYKU 293

The sun and substance
Admonish all, teach them too
Sun proclaims the day

MYKU 294

Look at cranes flying
Never sacrifice the good
Reaching for perfect

MYKU 295

On the river
Spider suspended on web
Serene cranes fly by

MYKU 296

Road trip remembered
Color up the mountain side
To snowcapped ridges

MYKU 297

The sun going down
A bat, a curious bird
Reluctant to learn

MYKU 298

Night is approaching
People talk and talk and talk
Words float on the sea

MYKU 299

November sails in
Across the Sea of Japan
I came to meet it

MYKU 300

I look, I listen
Try to receive the spirits
Then talk, write and paint

MYKU 301

In sunset colors
Black rocks jut out in water
Fishermen return

MYKU 302

Corner flower shop
Welcome sight in every town
Growing from sidewalk

MYKU 303

My eyes assaulted
Wires, gray stained patches lurking
Many red banners

MYKU 304

Clothes racks brown boxes
Vegetable bins beckon
Come in and buy now

MYKU 305

Children off to school
Salary men to the train
Merchants stacking wares

MYKU 306

All over the world
People are getting ready
Pursuing purpose

MYKU 307

Dark nobly trunks
Cherry trees in November
Shed leaves in motion

MYKU 308

The grass is still green
Soon all will be dried and brown
Crushed beneath my feet

MYKU 309

All leaves find a home
Decaying deep in the dirt
Content is the worm

MYKU 310

It's a horrid day
Maybe the fault is with you
Or with someone else

MYKU 311

Shaggy back peels off
The world is cruel and unkind
Yet still marvelous

MYKU 312

Life is a struggle
With ourselves and with others
The pine branch hangs down

MYKU 313

Take a walk about
Live life- don't talk about it
Moss on the tree bark

MYKU 314

Cool cascading stream
Walking across the cloud bridge
Mountain shaped wet rocks

MYKU 315

On the sunset
Turtles stacked up on turtles
Autumn leaves float past

MYKU 316

　　While maples turn red
　　November is acceptance
　　Pink camellias bloom

MYKU 317

　　Rosy petals fall
　　One by one on grassy ground
　　Minute by minute

MYKU 318

　　A trifling thing
　　Modesty in action
　　Petals in the air

Year's End

If knot will untie

Explore the many options

Reserve the cutting

MYKU 319

A blank temple wall
To draw cats you must see cats
The cat looks at me

MYKU 320

Bridge to the shrine sale
Crowds mingling amount venders
Hopeful of bargains

MYKU 321

Meeting on a price
Haggling is noble art
Don't disparage it

MYKU 322

Success for each side
Trudging off laden with bags
Time for a cold drink

MYKU 323

Red, yellow, blue, green
Banners show preparation
For tomorrow's fete

MYKU 324

Sometimes you release
No banking on tomorrow
Sometimes you must grab

MYKU 325

Time spent together
Meandering through the park
Tall buildings watching

MYKU 326

Falling Ginkgo leaves
Bending fingers together
Picking up the fruit

MYKU 327

Yellow grabs the eye
Red berries cry for notice
I turn and walk on

MYKU 328

Standing in the pond
The withered dried lotus leaves
People on the bridge

MYKU 329

Many small tan hats
Along a swampy river
Reflecting notions

MYKU 330

Shadows overhead
The year is quickly over
Cross the bridge slowly

MYKU 331

Sun, wind, cold, rain, moon
Swirling graceful patina
Goddess of mercy

MYKU 332

The bridge of shoppers
All bundled up bags in tow
My hands are empty

MYKU 333

Pay close attention
When you hold things in your hand
Fingers lose their grip

MYKU 334

Making my MYKUs
An esoteric whimsy
Transient markers

MYKU 335

Characters make words
City is many buildings
Many people too

MYKU 336

Among these structures
Our needs are met everyday
More people more buildings

MYKU 337

Cities or nature
Of which world do I belong
The nature of man

MYKU 338

Full moon mindfulness
The beauty is in the weeds
Take care to notice

MYKU 339

Listen completely
Mixed cultures same sun and moon
Effort looks not at results

MYKU 340

Ocean waves or plowed fields
Floating clouds or shifting rocks
Sunset or sunrise

MYKU 341

Calligraphy class
White sands of the ocean
Write prosperity

MYKU 342

The moon is behind
Clouds hover around the sky
But I am still here

MYKU 343

Three friends of winter
Lofty pine, plum, tall bamboo
Resilient steadfast

MYKU 344

The black pines struggle
Wind and rain shape beauty
When you speak use verbs

MYKU 345

She walks through the sun
In the market by the sea
Hungry for *ramen*

MYKU 346

Business, temple, park
Situation sets manner
Accordingly act

MYKU 347

Out of the forest
A wedding party appears
New obligations

MYKU 348

In between the leaves
Life happens down to our roots
Terra cotta pot

MYKU 349

Happiness, sadness
Feelings move as a liquid
Through flexible veins

MYKU 350

Augmenting the night
The band's passionate ardor
Evanescent sound

MYKU 351

Warm protective place
Brings the soul up the roots
Rest, water and light

MYKU 354

In caustic castles
On the ledge the council meets
Ground feeders below

MYKU 355

Following the path
Discovering in Japan
MYKU is my way

MYKU 356

Individuals
Have limitless connections
Give life poise not shape

MYKU 357

White face blackened teeth
For the stage in front of us
The mask for the role.

MYKU 358

Wearing new costumes
Smile for the camera
Being with nature

MYKU 359

I paint their portrait
While they take their picture
Maple leaf viewing

MYKU 360

Sharp stones in my shoes
A heavy briefcase in tow
Stop and look around

MYKU 361

Where are the tears now
Don't cry over anything
That won't weep for you

MYKU 362

Latent but unseen
A wise hawk hides its talons
Patience is humility

MYKU 363

With mind, without mind,
The space between the tunnels
My time in Japan

MYKU 364

On the low path
Found shimmering blue sea
Life hold surprises

MYKU 365

I fell down all year
But I got up every time
Daruma has two eyes

MYKU O

I Look I Listen
I receive the Spirits now
Then talk, write and paint

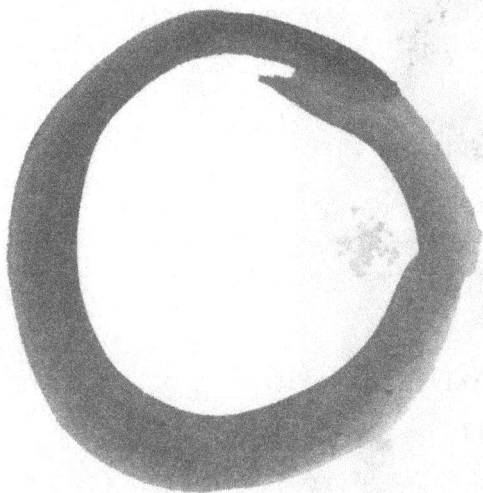

Afterword

Living in Japan Tanya Richey wrote over 400 Myku and painted hundreds of original images which capture the Spirit of Japan as she experienced it.

This book presents 371 of the poems she wrote during her two years in Japan. As her time in Japan was closing the question of where and how to present the work was on her mind. The was answer, inspired by a special cultural exchange art exhibition between Fredericksburg, Virginia and Schwetzingen, Germany. Visiting Tanya's gallery in Fredericksburg the German Mayor invited her to "Bring Fredericksburg to Schwetzingen".

Paintings of Fredericksburg, the spirit of Fredericksburg was packed into suitcases flying over the Atlantic so that people unable to make the physical journey to Virginia might still enjoy a cross-cultural experience.

The Spirit of Japan collection had therefor been named as soon as the opportunity for the adventure arose. Tanya was not going to Japan to learn painting in a Japanese style, she was already a master painter in her own right. Her intention was to visually capture the experiences of being in Japan and share her artist's view of another foreign land.

As she studied history, Japanese writing systems, geography, and tried to figure out how to get around the train system the collection began to form with Haiku- no, myku, at the center.

For the first time, her creative expression was centered around written words instead of painted images. Through daily painting she imprinted colors and shapes and experiences around her. Through daily writing her inner thoughts bleed into the colorful work she produced.

Tanya saw the Spirit of Japan collection reaching the world as a series of 12 books. Each volume is about 32pages and focuses on a single month and season.

The 12 volume Spirit of Japan book set was underway when Tanya's stage IV cancer was discovered, and the remaining year of her life focused on time with family and preparing all twelve books for publication. As chemo-therapy progressed we realized that monthly volumes were exactly what many patients needed. In times of medical peril and terminal stress you can't read a novel or complete a word search, but we noticed many patients found comfort or amusement flipping through the pages a book filled with colorful painting lined with three line flashed of poetry.

In response to requests for handheld book of poetry this collection presents the original set of numbered myku. One for each day of the year.

The MyKu Project

In June 2018 Tanya Richey passed on leaving a legacy of art and poetry around the world.

She believed that so many people go blindly past good parts of their life because we dream to big and devalue so much that is too small.

As a transient child she did not have the support networks modern society strives to afford every child or the fairness we want for every adult.

As a child she was too busy fitting into new schools, finding vending machines for breakfast, and not getting too attached because in a few months a Trailways bus would drop them off in a new town where she'd recycle the process.

She created a steady home for her own family and when her daughter went to school she was inspired to paint. Watercolors were cheap which meant her paintings could be terrible and one by one they became incredible.

Tanya called her Japanese inspired poetry MyKu because she knew they would never measure up to formal haiku but she did the best she could. She followed the syllable patter 5-7-5, retained themes of nature, and used "cutting words" in her observational poems.

Most of her life this extradentary woman created amazing work from sparse resources. Her supplies were imagination and tenacity.

She had moments of doubt in the middle of every painting and before the doors opened at every gallery show. Her way to push past the doubt was to turn the painting upside down for new perspective and have something small to work on in case no one came to the new show.

People did come, and her work was honored and collected.

"The fumy thing", she would say, "is often, the painting that I hate and want to bury in the back is the one everyone gushes over. It was just a folly."

We have to give ourselves space to create follies and the courage to share them with others before the insecure critic inside sucks us into a vacuumed.

The MyKu Project is a continuation of Tanya Richey's spirit of create. There are some guidelines to writing MyKu (Afterall they are stylized haiku) but the structure 5-7-5 is to focus your observations not restrict them.

Join the Journey!
Read the books!
Be inspired…
Go write a Myku!

Author Bio

Tanya M. Richey (1947-2018) was an American fine artist with paintings hanging in public, private and corporate collections around the world. In the 1990's she painted, taught, and exhibited her art in Europe, Egypt, and Soviet Russia

In the 1990's she directed a grant funded co-operative gallery while owning and operating her first independent gallery.

In the new millennium her original work continues across America, Germany, and Japan.

She believed in "elegant appreciation of nature through artistic pursuits such as poetry, paintings, and calligraphy."

"Painting is my way to center myself and interpret the world around me."

More by Tanya Richey

SPIRIT OF JAPAN
MyKu Ichi
MyKu Ni
MyKu San
MyKu Yon
MyKu Go
MyKu Roku
MyKu Nana
MyKu Hachi
MyKu Kyu
MyKu Ju
MyKu Ju-Ichi
MyKu Ju-Ni

SPIRIT OF FREDERICKSBURG
SPIRIT OF GERMANY

Availabe on Amazon
www.bairink.com
www.tmrart.com

Follow on Social Media

www.ingramcontent.com/pod-product-compliance
Lightning Source LLC
Chambersburg PA
CBHW031602040426
42452CB00006B/389